# *The Miraculous Journey of*
# EDWARD TULANE

1936

# *The Miraculous Journey of* EDWARD TULANE

KATE DICAMILLO

ILLUSTRATED BY BAGRAM IBATOULLINE

Long tail Books

**The Miraculous Journey of Edward Tulane**

Published by arrangement with Walker Books Limited, London SE11 5HJ.


ISBN 979-11-91343-90-8 14740

Longtail Books

*For Jane Resh Thomas,*

*who gave me the rabbit and told me his name*

The heart breaks and breaks
and lives by breaking.
It is necessary to go
through dark and deeper dark
and not to turn.

— from "The Testing-Tree," by Stanley Kunitz

# Chapter One

ONCE, IN A HOUSE ON EGYPT STREET, there lived a rabbit who was made almost **entire**ly of china.★ He had china arms and china legs, china **paw**s and a china head, a china **torso** and a china nose. His arms and legs were **joint**ed and joined by **wire** so that his china elbows and china knees could be bent, giving him much freedom of movement.

His ears were made of real rabbit fur, and beneath the fur, there were strong, **bendable** wires, which allowed the ears to be **arrange**d into poses that **reflect**ed the rabbit's mood—**jaunty**, tired, full of **ennui**. His tail, too, was made of real rabbit fur and was **fluffy** and soft and well

★ china 도자기.

shaped.

The rabbit's name was Edward Tulane, and he was tall. He **measure**d almost three feet★ from the **tip** of his ears to the tip of his feet; his eyes were painted a **penetrating** and **intelligent** blue.

In all, Edward Tulane felt himself to be an **exception**al **specimen**. Only his **whiskers** gave him **pause**. They were long and **elegant** (as they should be), but they were of uncertain **origin**. Edward felt quite strongly that they were not the whiskers of a rabbit. Whom the whiskers had belonged to **initial**ly—what **unsavory** animal—was a question that Edward could not **bear** to **consider** for too long. And so he did not. He **prefer**red, as a rule, not to think unpleasant thoughts.

Edward's **mistress** was a ten-year-old, dark-haired girl named Abilene Tulane, who thought almost as highly of Edward as Edward thought of himself. Each morning after she dressed herself for school, Abilene dressed Edward.

The china rabbit was in **possession** of an **extraordinary** **wardrobe** **compose**d of **handmade** silk suits, **custom** shoes **fashion**ed from the finest leather and designed **specific**ally for his rabbit feet, and a wide **array** of hats **equip**ped with

---

★ feet 길이의 단위 피트. 1피트는 약 30.48센티미터이다.

holes so that they could easily **fit** over Edward's large and **expressive** ears. Each pair of well-cut pants had a small pocket for Edward's gold pocket watch. Abilene **wound** this watch for him each morning.

"Now, Edward," she said to him after she had done winding the watch, "when the big hand is on the twelve and the little hand is on the three, I will come home to you."

She placed Edward on a chair in the **dining room** and **position**ed the chair so that Edward was looking out of the window and could see the path that **led** up to the Tulane front door. Abilene balanced the watch on his left leg. She kissed the tips of his ears, and then she left and Edward spent the day **staring** out at Egypt Street, listening to the **tick** of his watch and waiting.

Of all the seasons of the year, the rabbit most preferred winter, for the sun set early then and the dining room windows became dark and Edward could see his own **reflection** in the glass. And what a reflection it was! What an elegant **figure** he **cut**! Edward never **ceased** to be amazed at his own fineness.

In the evening, Edward sat at the dining-room table with the other members of the Tulane family: Abilene; her mother and father; and Abilene's grandmother, who was called Pellegrina. True, Edward's ears **barely** cleared the **tabletop**, and true also, he spent the **duration** of the meal staring straight ahead at nothing but the bright and **blind**ing white of the **tablecloth**. But he was there, a rabbit at the table.

Abilene's parents found it **charming** that Abilene considered Edward real, and that she sometimes **request**ed that a **phrase** or story be repeated because Edward had not heard it.

"Papa," Abilene would say, "I'm afraid that Edward didn't catch that last bit."

Abilene's father would then turn in the direction of Edward's ears and speak slowly, repeating what he had just said for the **benefit** of the china rabbit. Edward **pretend**ed, out of **courtesy** to Abilene, to listen. But, in truth, he was not very interested in what people had to say. And also, he did not care for Abilene's parents and their **condescend**ing manner toward him. All adults, in fact, condescended to him.

Only Abilene's grandmother spoke to him as Abilene did, as one equal to another. Pellegrina was very old. She had a large, sharp nose and bright, black eyes that **shone** like dark stars. It was Pellegrina who was **responsible** for Edward's **existence**. It was she who had **commission**ed his making, she who had ordered his silk suits and his pocket watch, his jaunty hats and his bendable ears, his fine leather shoes and his jointed arms and legs, all from a master **craftsman** in her native France. It was Pellegrina who had given him as a gift to Abilene on her seventh birthday.

And it was Pellegrina who came each night to **tuck** Abilene into her bed and Edward into his.

"Will you tell us a story, Pellegrina?" Abilene asked her grandmother each night.

"Not tonight, lady," said Pellegrina.

"When?" asked Abilene. "What night?"

"Soon," said Pellegrina. "Soon there will be a story."

And then she turned off the light, and Edward and Abilene **lay** in the dark of the bedroom.

"I love you, Edward," Abilene said each night after Pellegrina had left. She said those words and then she waited, almost as if she expected Edward to say something **in return**.

Edward said nothing. He said nothing because, of course, he could not speak. He lay in his small bed next to Abilene's large one. He stared up at the ceiling and listened to the sound of her breath entering and leaving her body, knowing that soon she would be asleep. Because Edward's eyes were painted on and he could not close them, he was always awake.

Sometimes, if Abilene put him into his bed on his

side instead of on his back, he could see through the **cracks** in the curtains and out into the dark night. On clear nights, the stars shone, and their **pinprick** light **comfort**ed Edward in a way that he could not quite understand. Often, he stared at the stars all night until the dark finally **gave way** to **dawn.**

# Chapter Two

AND IN THIS MANNER, EDWARD'S DAYS passed, one into the other. Nothing **remarkable** happened. Oh, there was the **occasional** small, **domestic** drama. Once, while Abilene was at school, the neighbor's dog, a male **brindled** boxer* **inexplicably** named Rosie, came into the house uninvited and un**announced** and lifted his leg on the **dining-room** table, spraying the white **tablecloth** with **urine**. He then **trotted** over and **sniffed** Edward, and before Edward even had time to **consider** the **implication**s of being sniffed by a dog, he was in Rosie's mouth and Rosie was shaking him back and forth **vigorously**, **growl**ing and **drool**ing.

---

★ **boxer** 복서. 코가 납작하고 몸집이 큰 개. 싸울 때 권투선수처럼 앞발로 때리는 데에서 이름이 유래했다.

**Fortunately**, Abilene's mother walked past the dining room and **witnessed** Edward's **suffer**ing.

"Drop it!" she shouted to Rosie.

And Rosie, surprised into **obedience**, did as he was told.

Edward's silk suit was **stain**ed with drool and his head **ached** for several days afterward, but it was his **ego** that had suffered the most damage. Abilene's mother had **refer**red to him as "it," and she was more **outraged** at the dog urine on her tablecloth than she was about the **indignities** that Edward had suffered at the **jaws** of Rosie.

And then there was the time that a **maid**, new to the Tulane **household** and **eager** to **impress** her **employer**s with her **diligence**, came upon Edward sitting on his chair in the dining room.

"What's this bunny★ doing here?" she said out loud.

Edward did not care at all for the word *bunny*. He found it **derogatory** in the **extreme**.

The maid bent over him and looked into his eyes.

"Humph," she said. She stood back up. She put her hands on her hips. "I **reckon** you're just like every other thing in this house, something needing to be cleaned and **dusted**."

---

★**bunny** (유아어) 토끼.

"Drop it!" she shouted to Rosie.

And so the maid **vacuumed** Edward Tulane. She **sucked** each of his long ears up the vacuum-cleaner hose. She **pawed** at his clothes and **beat** his tail. She dusted his face with **brutality** and **efficiency**. And in her **zeal** to clean him, she vacuumed Edward's gold pocket watch right off his **lap**. The watch went into the **maw** of the vacuum cleaner with a **distressing** ***clank*** that the maid did not even seem to hear.

When she was done, she put the dining-room chair back at the table, and uncertain about exactly where Edward belonged, she finally decided to **shove** him in among the dolls on a shelf in Abilene's bedroom.

"That's right," said the maid. "There you go."

She left Edward on the shelf at a most **awkward** and **inhuman angle**—his nose was actually touching his knees—and he waited there, with the dolls **twittering** and **giggling** at him like a **flock** of **demented** and unfriendly birds, until Abilene came home from school and found him missing and ran from room to room calling his name.

"Edward!" she shouted. "Edward!"

There was no way, of course, for him to let her know where he was, no way for him to answer her. He could only sit and wait.

When Abilene found him, she held him close, so close

that Edward could feel her heart beating, **leap**ing almost out of her chest in its **agitation**.

"Edward," she said, "oh, Edward. I love you. I never want you to be away from me."

The rabbit, too, was experiencing a great emotion. But it was not love. It was **annoyance** that he had been so **mightily inconvenience**d, that he had been handled by the maid as **cavalier**ly as an **inanimate** object—a serving bowl, say, or a teapot. The only **satisfaction** to be had from the whole **affair** was that the new maid was **dismissed immediately**.

Edward's pocket watch was **located** later, deep within the **bowel**s of the vacuum cleaner, **dent**ed, but still in working condition; it was returned to him by Abilene's father, who presented it with a **mocking bow**.

"Sir Edward," he said. "Your **timepiece**, I believe?"

The Rosie Affair and the Vacuum-Cleaner **Incident**—those were the great dramas of Edward's life until the night of Abilene's eleventh birthday when, at the dinner table, as the cake was being **serve**d, the ship was **mention**ed.

# Chapter Three

SHE IS CALLED THE *QUEEN MARY,*" SAID Abilene's father, "and you and your mama and I shall sail on her all the way to London."

"What about Pellegrina?" said Abilene.

"I will not go," said Pellegrina. "I will stay."

Edward, of course, was not listening. He found the talk around the dinner table **excruciatingly dull**; in fact, he made a point of *not* listening if he could help it. But then Abilene did something **unusual**, something that **forced** him to pay **attention**. As the talk about the ship continued, Abilene reached for Edward and took him from his chair and stood him in her **lap**.

"And what about Edward?" she said, her voice high and uncertain.

"What about him, darling?" said her mother.

"Will Edward be sailing on the *Queen Mary* with us?"

"Well, of course, if you wish, although you are getting a little old for such things as china rabbits."

"**Nonsense**," said Abilene's father **jovial**ly. "Who would **protect** Abilene if Edward was not there?"

From the **vantage** point of Abilene's lap, Edward could see the whole table **spread** out before him in a way that he never could when he was seated in his own chair. He looked upon the **glitter**ing **array** of **silverware** and glasses and plates. He saw the **amused** and **condescend**ing looks of Abilene's parents. And then his eyes met Pellegrina's.

She was looking at him in the way a **hawk hang**ing lazily in the air might study a mouse on the ground. Perhaps the rabbit fur on Edward's ears and tail, and the **whisker**s on his nose had some **dim** memory of being hunted, for a **shiver** went through him.

"Yes," said Pellegrina without taking her eyes off Edward, "who would watch over Abilene if the rabbit were not there?"

That night, when Abilene asked, as she did every night, if there would be a story, Pellegrina said, "Tonight, lady, there will be a story."

Abilene sat up in bed. "I think that Edward needs to sit here with me," she said, "so that he can hear the story too."

"I think that is best," said Pellegrina. "Yes, I think that the rabbit must hear the story."

Abilene picked Edward up, sat him next to her in bed, and **arranged** the covers around him; then she said to Pellegrina, "We are ready now."

"So," said Pellegrina. She **coughed**. "And so. The story begins with a princess."

"A beautiful princess?" Abilene asked.

"A very beautiful princess."

"How beautiful?"

"You must listen," said Pellegrina. "It is all in the story."

# CHAPTER FOUR

ONCE THERE WAS A PRINCESS WHO WAS very beautiful. She **shone** as bright as the stars on a **moonless** night. But what difference did it make that she was beautiful? None. No difference."

"Why did it make no difference?" asked Abilene.

"Because," said Pellegrina, "she was a princess who loved no one and cared nothing for love, even though there were many who loved her."

At this point in her story, Pellegrina stopped and looked right at Edward. She **stared** deep into his painted-on eyes, and again, Edward felt a **shiver** go through him.

"And so," said Pellegrina, still staring at Edward.

"What happened to the princess?" said Abilene.

"And so," said Pellegrina, turning back to Abilene,

"the king, her father, said that the princess must marry; and soon after this, a prince came from a **neighboring** kingdom and he saw the princess, and **immediately** he loved her. He gave her a ring of pure gold. He placed it on her finger. He said these words to her: 'I love you.' But do you know what the princess did?"

Abilene shook her head.

"She **swallowed** the ring. She took it from her finger and swallowed it. She said, 'That is what I think of love.' And she ran from the prince. She left the castle and went deep into the woods. And so."

"And so what?" said Abilene. "What happened then?"

"And so, the princess became lost in the woods. She **wandered** for many days. Finally, she came to a little **hut**, and she knocked on the door. She said, 'Let me in; I am cold.'

"There was no answer.

"She knocked again. She said, 'Let me in; I am hungry.'

"A terrible voice answered her. The voice said, 'Enter if you must.'

"The beautiful princess entered, and she saw a **witch** sitting at a table counting pieces of gold.

"'Three thousand, six hundred and twenty-two,' said the witch.

"'I am lost,' said the beautiful princess.

"Because," said Pellegrina, "she was a princess who loved no one and cared nothing for love, even though there were many who loved her."

"'What of it?' said the witch. 'Three thousand, six hundred and twenty-three.'

"'I am hungry,' said the princess.

"'Not my **concern**,' said the witch. 'Three thousand, six hundred and twenty-four.'

"'But I am a beautiful princess,' said the princess.

"'Three thousand, six hundred and twenty-five,' replied the witch.

"'My father,' said the princess, 'is a powerful king. You must help me or there will be **consequences**.'

"'Consequences?' said the witch. She looked up from her gold. She stared at the princess. 'You **dare** to talk to me of consequences? Very well, then, we will speak of consequences: tell me the name of the one you love.'

"'Love!' said the princess. She **stamp**ed her foot. 'Why must everyone always speak of love?'

"'Whom do you love?' said the witch. 'You must tell me the name.'

"'I love no one,' said the princess proudly.

"'You disappoint me,' said the witch. She raised her hand and said one word: 'Farthfigery.'

"And the beautiful princess was changed into a warthog.★

★ **warthog** [동물] 혹멧돼지.

"'What have you done to me?' **squeal**ed the princess.

"'Talk to me of consequences now, will you?' said the witch, and she went back to counting her pieces of gold. 'Three thousand, six hundred and twenty-six,' said the witch as the warthog princess ran from the hut and out again into the forest.

"The king's men were in the forest too. And what were they looking for? A beautiful princess. And so when they came upon an ugly warthog, they shot it immediately. Pow!★"

"No," said Abilene.

"Yes," said Pellegrina. "The men took the warthog back to the castle and the cook **slit** open its **belly** and inside it she found a ring of pure gold. There were many hungry people in the castle that night and all of them were waiting to be **fed**. So the cook put the ring on her finger and finished **butcher**ing the warthog. And the ring that the beautiful princess had swallowed shone on the cook's hand as she did her work. The end."

"The end?" said Abilene **indignant**ly.

"Yes," said Pellegrina, "the end."

"But it can't be."

"Why can't it be?"

---

★ pow 빵 하는 소리.

"Because it came too quickly. Because no one is living happily ever after, that's why."

"Ah, and so." Pellegrina **nodded**. She was quiet for a moment. "But answer me this: how can a story end happily if there is no love? But. Well. It is late. And you must go to sleep."

Pellegrina took Edward from Abilene. She put him in his bed and pulled the sheet up to his whiskers. She **leaned** close to him. She **whispered**, "You disappoint me."

After the old lady left, Edward **lay** in his small bed and stared up at the ceiling. The story, he thought, had been **pointless**. But then most stories were. He thought of the princess and how she had become a warthog. How **gruesome**! How **grotesque**! What a terrible **fate**!

"Edward," said Abilene, "I love you. I don't care how old I get, I will always love you."

Yes, yes, thought Edward.

He continued to stare up at the ceiling. He was **agitated** for some reason that he could not name. He wished that Pellegrina had put him on his side so that he might look at the stars.

And then he remembered Pellegrina's **description** of the beautiful princess. She shone as bright as the stars on a moonless night. For some reason, Edward found **comfort** in these words and he repeated them to himself—*as bright as the stars on a moonless night, as bright as the stars on a moonless night*—over and over until, at last, the first light of **dawn** appeared.

# Chapter Five

THE HOUSE ON EGYPT STREET BECAME **frantic** with activity as the Tulane family prepared for their **voyage** to England. Edward **possessed** a small trunk, and Abilene packed it for him, filling it with his finest suits and several of his best hats and three pairs of shoes, all so that he might **cut a** fine **figure** in London. Before she placed each **outfit** in the trunk, she **display**ed it to him.

"Do you like this shirt with this suit?" she asked him.

Or "Would you like to wear your black **derby**? You look very handsome in it. Shall we pack it?"

And then, finally, on a bright Saturday morning in May, Edward and Abilene and Mr. and Mrs. Tulane were all onboard the ship, standing at the **railing.** Pellegrina was at the **dock**. On her head, she wore a **floppy** hat **strung** around with flowers. She stared straight at Edward. Her dark eyes **glow**ed.

"Goodbye," Abilene shouted to her grandmother. "I love you."

The ship pulled away from the dock. Pellegrina waved to Abilene.

"Goodbye, lady," she called, "goodbye."

Edward felt something **damp** in his ears. Abilene's tears, he **suppose**d. He wished that she would not hold him so tight. To be **clutch**ed so **fierce**ly often **result**ed in **wrinkle**d clothing. Finally, all the people on land, including Pellegrina, disappeared. Edward, for one, was **relieve**d to see the last of her.

As was to be expected, Edward Tulane **exact**ed much **attention** on board the ship.

"What a **singular** rabbit," said an elderly lady with three strings of pearls wrapped around her neck. She bent down to look more closely at Edward.

"Thank you," said Abilene.

Several little girls on board gave Edward deep **glances** full of **longing**. They asked Abilene if they might hold him.

"No," said Abilene, "I'm afraid that he's not the kind of rabbit who likes to be held by strangers."

Two young boys, brothers named Martin and Amos, took a **particular** interest in Edward.

"What does he do?" Martin asked Abilene on their second day at sea. He pointed at Edward, who was sitting on a **deck** chair* with his long legs stretched in front of him.

"He doesn't do anything," said Abilene.

"Does he **wind** up somewhere?" asked Amos.

"No," said Abilene, "he does not wind up."

"What's the point of him then?" said Martin.

"The point is that he is Edward," said Abilene.

"That's not much of a point," said Amos.

"It's not," agreed Martin. And then, after a long **thoughtful pause**, he said, "I wouldn't let anybody dress me like that."

"Me neither," said Amos.

"Do his clothes come off?" asked Martin.

"Of course they do," said Abilene. "He has many different outfits. And he has his own **pajamas** too. They are made of silk."

Edward, as usual, was **disregard**ing the conversation. A **breeze** was blowing in off the sea, and the silk scarf wrapped around his neck **billow**ed out behind him. On

---

* **deck chair** 갑판 의자. 휴대용 접이식 의자.

his head, he wore a **straw boater**. The rabbit was thinking that he must look quite **dashing**.

It came as a total surprise to him when he was **grab**bed off the deck chair and first his scarf, and then his jacket and pants, were **rip**ped from his body. Edward saw his pocket watch hit the deck of the ship and roll **merrily** toward Abilene's feet.

"Look at him," said Martin. "He's even got **underwear**." He held Edward **aloft** so that Amos could see.

"Take it off," shouted Amos.

"NO!!!!" screamed Abilene.

Martin removed Edward's underwear.

Edward was paying attention now. He was **mortified**. He was completely **naked except** for the hat on his head, and the other **passenger**s onboard the ship were looking at him, directing **curious** and **embarrass**ed glances his way.

"Give him to me," screamed Abilene. "He's mine."

"No," said Amos to Martin, "give him to *me*." He **clap**ped his hands together and then held them open. "Toss him," he said.

"Please," cried Abilene. "Don't throw him. He's made of china. He'll break."

Martin threw Edward.

And Edward sailed naked through the air. Only a moment ago, the rabbit had thought that being naked in front of a **shipload** of strangers was the worst thing that could happen to him. But he was wrong. It was much worse being tossed, in the same naked state, from the hands of one **grubby**, laughing boy to another.

Amos caught Edward and held him up, displaying him **triumphant**ly.

"Throw him back," called Martin.

Amos raised his arm, but just as he was getting ready to throw Edward, Abilene **tackled** him, **shoving** her head into his stomach, and **upset**ting the boy's **aim**.

So it was that Edward did not go flying back into the dirty hands of Martin.

Instead, Edward Tulane went **overboard**.

# Chapter Six

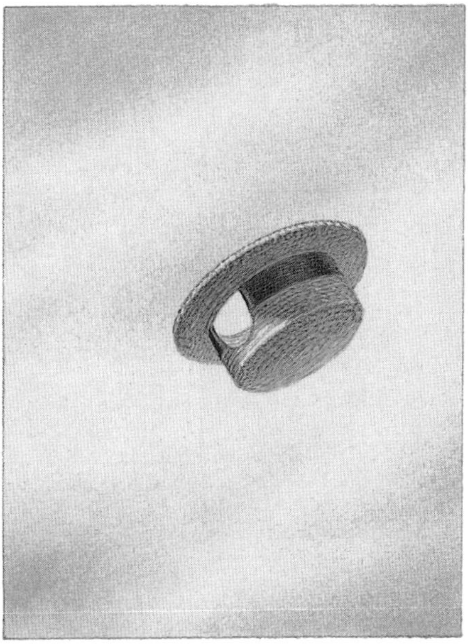

HOW DOES A CHINA RABBIT DIE?

Can a china rabbit **drown**?

Is my hat still on my head?

These were the questions that Edward asked himself as he went sailing out over the blue sea. The sun was high in the sky, and from what seemed to be a very long way away, Edward heard Abilene call his name.

"Edwaaarrd," she shouted, "come back."

Come back? Of all the **ridiculous** things to shout, thought Edward.

As he **tumbled**, ears over tail through the air, he managed to catch one last **glimpse** of Abilene. She was standing on the deck of the ship, holding on to the **railing** with one hand. In her other hand was a lamp—no, it was

He sank and sank and sank.

a ball of fire; no, Edward realized, it was his gold pocket watch that Abilene held in her hand; she was holding it up high, and it was **reflect**ing the light of the sun.

My pocket watch, he thought. I need that.

And then Abilene disappeared from view and the rabbit hit the water with such **tremendous force** that his hat blew off his head.

That answers that question, thought Edward as he watched the hat dance away on the wind.

And then he began to **sink**.

He sank and sank and sank. He kept his eyes open the whole time. Not because he was brave, but because he had no choice. His painted-on eyes **witness**ed the blue water turning to green and then to blue again. They watched as it finally became as black as night.

Edward went down and down. He said to himself, If I am going to drown, certainly I would have done so by now.

Far above him, the ocean liner,* with Abilene **aboard** it, sailed **blithe**ly on; and the china rabbit landed, finally, on the ocean floor, face down; and there, with his head in the **muck**, he experienced his first **genuine** and true emotion.

Edward Tulane was afraid.

---

★ ocean liner 원양 정기선.

# Chapter Seven

HE TOLD HIMSELF THAT CERTAINLY Abilene would come and find him. This, Edward thought, is much like waiting for Abilene to come home from school. I will **pretend** that I am in the **dining room** of the house on Egypt Street, waiting for the little hand to move to the three and the big hand to land on the twelve. If only I had my watch, then I would know for sure. But it doesn't matter; she will be here soon, very soon.

Hours passed. And then days. And weeks. And months.

Abilene did not come.

Edward, for lack of anything better to do, began to think. He thought about the stars. He remembered what they looked like from his bedroom window.

What made them shine so brightly, he **wonder**ed, and were they still shining somewhere even though he could not see them? Never in my life, he thought, have I been **further** away from the stars than I am now.

He **consider**ed, too, the **fate** of the beautiful princess who had become a warthog. Why had she become a warthog? Because the ugly **witch** had turned her into one—that was why.

And then the rabbit thought about Pellegrina. He felt, in some way that he could not explain to himself, that she was **responsible** for what had happened to him. It was almost as if it was she, and not the boys, who had thrown Edward **overboard**.

She was like the witch in the story. No, she *was* the witch in the story. True, she did not turn him into a warthog, but just the same she was **punish**ing him, although for what he could not say.

On the two hundred and ninety-seventh day of Edward's **ordeal**, a storm came. The storm was so powerful that it lifted Edward off the ocean floor and **led** him in a crazy, wild and **spin**ning dance. The water **pummel**ed him and lifted him up and **shoved** him back down.

Help! thought Edward.

The storm, in its **ferocity**, actually **flung** him all the way out of the sea; and the rabbit **glimpsed**, for a moment, the light of an angry and **bruised** sky; the wind **rush**ed through his ears. It sounded to him like Pellegrina laughing. But before he had time to **appreciate** being above water, he was tossed back down into the **depth**s. Up and down, back and forth he went until the storm **wore** itself **out**, and Edward saw that he was beginning, again, his slow **descent** to the ocean floor.

Oh, help me, he thought. I can't go back there. Help me.

But still, down he went. Down, down, down.

And then, suddenly, the great, wide net of a fisherman reached out and **grab**bed the rabbit. The net lifted him higher and higher until there was an almost **unbearable explosion** of light and Edward was back in the world, lying on the **deck** of a ship, **surround**ed by fish.

"Eh, what's this?" said a voice.

"Ain't★ no fish," said another voice. "That's for sure."

The light was so **brilliant** that it was hard for Edward to see. But finally, shapes appeared out of the light, and then faces. And Edward realized that he was looking up at two men, one young and one old.

---

★ ain't (구어) am[are, is] not의 단축형.

"Looks like some toy," said the **grizzled** old man. He bent and picked Edward up and held him by his front **paws**, considering him. "A rabbit, I **reckon**. It's got **whiskers**. And rabbit ears, or the shape of rabbit ears at least."

"Yeah, sure, a rabbit toy," said the younger man, and he turned away.

"I'll take it home to Nellie. Let her fix it up and **set it to rights**. Give it to some child."

The old man placed Edward carefully on a **crate**, **position**ing him so that he was sitting up and could look out at the sea. Edward appreciated the **courtesy** of this small gesture, but he was **heartily** sick of the ocean and would have been satisfied never to set eyes on it again.

"There you go," said the old man. As they made their way back to **shore**, Edward felt the sun on his face and the wind blowing through the little bit of fur left on his ears, and something filled his chest, a wonderful feeling.

He was glad to be alive.

"Look at that rabbit," the old man said. "Looks like it's enjoying the ride, don't it?"

"A-yep," said the young man.

In fact, Edward Tulane was so happy to be back among the living that he did not even take **umbrage** at being **referred** to as "it."

# Chapter Eight

ON LAND, THE OLD FISHERMAN stopped to **light** a **pipe**, and then, with the pipe **clench**ed between his teeth, he walked home, carrying Edward **atop** his left shoulder as if he were a **conquer**ing hero. The fisherman balanced him there, placing a **callused** hand at Edward's back. He talked to him in a soft, low voice as they walked.

"You'll like Nellie, you will," said the old man. "She's had her sadness, but she's an all-right girl."

Edward looked at the small town **blanketed** in **dusk**: a **jumble** of buildings **huddle**d together, the ocean stretching out in front of it all; and he thought that he would like anything and anybody that was not at the bottom of the sea.

"Hello, Lawrence," called a woman from the front of a shop. "What have you got?"

"Fresh catch," said the fisherman, "fresh rabbit from the sea." He lifted his cap to the lady and kept walking.

"There you are, now," said the fisherman. He took the pipe out of his mouth and pointed with the stem of it at a star in the purpling sky. "There's your North Star★ right there. Don't never have to be lost when you know where that **fellow** is."

Edward **considere**d the brightness of the small star.

Do they all have names? he **wondere**d.

"Listen at me," said the fisherman, "talking to a toy. Oh, well. Here we are, then." And with Edward still on his shoulder, the fisherman walked up a stone-lined path and into a little green house.

"Look here, Nellie," he said. "I've brought you something from the sea."

"I don't want nothing from the sea," came a voice.

"Aw, now, don't be like that, Nell. Come and see, then."

An old woman stepped out of the kitchen, wiping her hands on an **apron**. When she saw Edward, she dropped the apron and **clapp**ed her hands together and said, "Oh,

---

★ North Star 북극성.

"She's beautiful," breathed Nellie.

Lawrence, you brung★ me a rabbit."

"Direct from the sea," said Lawrence. He took Edward off his shoulder and stood him up on the floor and held on to his hands and made him take a deep **bow** in the direction of Nellie.

"Oh," said Nellie, "here." She clapped her hands together again and Lawrence passed Edward to her.

Nellie held the rabbit out in front of her and looked him over from tip to toe. She smiled. "Have you ever in your life seen anything so fine?" she said.

Edward felt **immediately** that Nellie was a very **discerning** woman.

"She's beautiful," breathed Nellie.

For a moment, Edward was **confused**. Was there some other object of beauty in the room?

"What will I call her?"

"Susanna?" said Lawrence.

"Just right," said Nellie. "Susanna." She looked deep into Edward's eyes. "First off, Susanna will need some clothes, won't she?"

★ **brung** bring의 과거분사형인 brought의 사투리.

# Chapter Nine

AND SO EDWARD TULANE BECAME Susanna. Nellie **sew**ed several **outfit**s for him: a pink dress with **ruffle**s for special **occasion**s, a simple shift★ **fashion**ed out of a flower-covered cloth for everyday use, and a long white gown made of **cotton** for Edward to sleep in. In addition, she remade his ears, **strip**ping them of the few pieces of fur that remained and designing him a new pair.

"Oh," she told him when she was done, "you look lovely."

He was **horrified** at first. He was, after all, a boy rabbit. He did not want to be dressed as a girl. And the outfits, even the special-occasion dress, were so simple,

★ **shift** 시프트 원피스. 치마폭이 넓지 않은 단순한 원피스.

so plain. They lacked the **elegance** and **artistry** of his real clothes. But then Edward remembered **lying** on the ocean floor, the **muck** in his face, the stars so far away, and he said to himself, What difference does it make really? Wearing a dress won't hurt me.

Besides, life in the little green house with the fisherman and his wife was sweet. Nellie loved to bake, and so she spent her day in the kitchen. She put Edward on the counter and **leaned** him up against the **flour canister** and **arranged** his dress around his knees. She bent his ears so that he could hear well.

And then she set to work, **kneading dough** for bread and rolling out dough for cookies and pies. The kitchen soon filled with the smell of baking bread and with the sweet smells of cinnamon★ and sugar and cloves.✱ The windows **steamed** up. And while Nellie worked, she talked.

She told Edward about her children: her daughter, Lolly, who was a **secretary**; and her boys: Ralph, who was in the army; and Raymond, who had died of pneumonia❋ when he was only five years old.

"He **drowned** inside of himself," said Nellie. "It

---

★ cinnamon 계피.
✱ clove 정향. 정향나무의 꽃봉오리를 말린 향료.
❋ pneumonia 폐렴.

is a **horrible**, terrible thing, the worst thing, to watch somebody you love die right in front of you and not be able to do nothing about it. I dream about him most nights."

Nellie wiped at her tears with the back of her hands. She smiled at Edward.

"I **suppose** you think I'm **daft**, talking to a toy. But it seems to me that you are listening, Susanna."

And Edward was surprised to discover that he was listening. Before, when Abilene talked to him, everything had seemed so boring, so **pointless**. But now, the stories Nellie told **struck** him as the most important thing in the world and he listened as if his life depended on what she said. It made him wonder if some of the muck from the ocean floor had got inside his china head and damaged him **somehow**.

In the evening, Lawrence came home from the sea and there was dinner and Edward sat at the table with the fisherman and his wife. He sat in an old wooden high chair; and while at first he was **mortified** (a high chair, after all, was a chair designed for babies, not for elegant rabbits), he soon became used to it. He liked being up high, looking out over the table instead of **staring** at the **tablecloth** as he had at the Tulane **household**. He liked feeling like a part of things.

Every night after dinner, Lawrence said that he

thought he would go out and get some fresh air and that maybe Susanna would like to come with him. He placed Edward on his shoulder as he had that first night when he walked him through town, bringing him home to Nellie.

They went outside and Lawrence **lit** his **pipe** and held Edward there on his shoulder; and if the night was clear, Lawrence said the names of the **constellation**s one at a time, Andromeda,★ Pegasus,✻ pointing at them with the stem of his pipe. Edward loved looking up at the stars, and he loved the sounds of the constellation names. They were sweet in his ears.

Sometimes, though, staring up at the night sky, Edward remembered Pellegrina, saw again her dark and **glow**ing eyes, and a **chill** would go through him.

Warthogs, he would think. **Witch**es.

But Nellie, before she put him to bed each night, sang Edward a **lullaby**, a song about a mockingbird❋ that did not sing and a diamond ring that would not **shine**, and the sound of Nellie's voice **sooth**ed the rabbit and he forgot about Pellegrina.

Life, for a very long time, was sweet.

And then Lawrence and Nellie's daughter came for a visit.

---

★ **Andromeda** [천문] 안드로메다자리.
✻ **Pegasus** [천문] 페가수스자리.
❋ **mockingbird** [조류] 흉내지빠귀.

# Chapter Ten

LOLLY WAS A **LUMPY** WOMAN WHO spoke too loudly and who wore too much lipstick. She entered the house and **immediately spotted** Edward sitting on the living-room **couch.**

"What's this?" she said. She put down her suitcase and picked Edward up by one foot. She held him **upside down.**

"That's Susanna," said Nellie.

"Susanna!" shouted Lolly. She gave Edward a shake.

His dress was up over his head and he could see nothing. Already, he had formed a deep and **abiding hatred** for Lolly.

"Your father found her," said Nellie. "She came up in a net and she didn't have no clothes on her, so I made her some dresses."

"Have you gone **skivvy**?" shouted Lolly. "Rabbits don't need clothes."

"Well," said Nellie. Her voice shook. "This one seemed to."

Lolly tossed Edward back on the couch. He landed face down with his arms over his head and his dress still over his face, and he stayed that way through dinner.

"Why have you got out that old high chair?" shouted Lolly.

"Oh, don't pay it no mind," said Nellie. "Your father was just **gluing** on a missing piece, wasn't you, Lawrence?"

"That's right," said Lawrence, without looking up from his plate.

Of course, after dinner Edward did not go outside and stand beneath the stars to have a smoke with Lawrence. And Nellie, for the first time since Edward had been with her, did not sing him a **lullaby**. In fact, Edward was **ignored** and forgotten about until the next morning, when Lolly picked him up again and pulled his dress down away from his face and stared him in the eye.

"Got the old **folks bewitched**, don't you?" said Lolly. "I heard the talk in town. That they've been treating you like a rabbit child."

Edward stared back at Lolly. Her lipstick was a bright and bloody red. He felt a cold **breeze** blow through the room.

Was a door open somewhere?

"Well, you don't fool me," she said. She gave him a shake. "We'll be taking a trip together, you and me."

Holding Edward by the ears, Lolly marched into the kitchen and **shoved** him face-down in the **garbage** can.

"Ma!" Lolly shouted, "I'm taking the truck. I'm going to head on out and do some **errands**."

"Oh," came Nellie's **tremulous** voice, "that's wonderful, dear. Goodbye, then."

Goodbye, thought Edward as Lolly **haul**ed the garbage can out to the truck.

"Goodbye," Nellie called again, louder this time.

Edward felt a sharp pain somewhere deep inside his china chest.

For the first time, his heart called out to him.

It said two words: Nellie. Lawrence.

# Chapter Eleven

EDWARD **ENDED UP** AT THE **DUMP**. HE lay on top of orange **peels**, coffee **grounds**, **rancid** bacon and rubber tires. The first night, he was at the top of the **garbage heap**, and so he was able to look up at the stars and find **comfort** in their light.

In the morning, a short man came climbing through the trash and **rubble**. He stopped when he was standing on top of the highest pile. He put his hands under his **armpits** and **flapped** his elbows.

The man **crowed** loudly. He shouted, "Who am I? I'm Ernest, Ernest who is king of the world. How can I be king of the world? Because I am king of garbages. And garbages is what the world is made of. Ha. Ha, ha! **Therefore**, I am Ernest, Ernest who is king of the world."

He crowed again.

Edward was **inclined** to agree with Ernest's **assessment** of the world being made of garbage, especially after his second day at the dump, when a **load** of trash was **deposit**ed directly on top of him. He lay there, **buried** alive. He could not see the sky. He could not see the stars. He could see nothing.

What kept Edward going, what gave him hope, was thinking of how he would find Lolly and **exact** his **revenge**. He would pick *her* up by the ears! He would bury *her* under a mountain of trash!

But after almost forty days and nights had passed, the weight and the smell of the garbage above and below him clouded Edward's thoughts, and soon he **gave up** thinking about revenge and **gave in** to **despair**. It was worse, much worse, than being buried at sea. It was worse because Edward was a different rabbit now. He couldn't say how he was different; he just knew that he was. He remembered, again, Pellegrina's story about the princess who had loved nobody. The **witch** turned her into a warthog *because* she loved nobody. He understood that now.

He heard Pellegrina say: "You disappoint me."

Why? he asked her. Why do I disappoint you?

But he knew the answer to that question too. It was

because he had not loved Abilene enough. And now she was gone from him. And he would never be able to make it right. And Nellie and Lawrence were gone too. He missed them terribly. He wanted to be with them.

The rabbit wondered if that was love.

Day after day passed, and Edward was **aware** of time passing only because every morning he could hear Ernest performing his **dawn ritual**, **cackling** and crowing about being king of the world.

On his one hundred and eightieth day at the dump, **salvation** arrived for Edward in a most **unusual** form. The garbage around him **shift**ed, and the rabbit heard the **sniffing** and **pant**ing of a dog. Then came the **frenzied** sound of digging. The garbage shifted again, and suddenly, **miraculous**ly, the beautiful, buttery light of late afternoon shone on Edward's face.

# Chapter Twelve

EDWARD DID NOT HAVE MUCH TIME to **savor** the light, for the dog suddenly appeared above him, dark and **shaggy**, blocking his view. Edward was pulled out of the garbage by his ears, dropped, and then picked up again, this time around the middle, and shaken back and forth with **a great deal of ferocity**.

The little dog **growl**ed deep in its **throat** and then dropped Edward again and looked him in the eye. Edward **stare**d back.

"Hey, get out of here, you dog!" It was Ernest, king of **garbages** and **therefore** king of the world.

The dog **grab**bed Edward by his pink dress and took off, running.

"That's mine, that's mine, all garbages is mine!"

Ernest shouted. "You come back here!"

But the little dog did not stop.

The sun was shining and Edward felt **exhilarated**. Who, having known him before, would have thought that he could be so happy now, **crusted** over with garbage, wearing a dress, held in the **slobbery** mouth of a dog and being **chased** by a madman?

But he was happy.

The dog ran and ran until they reached a railroad track. They crossed over the tracks, and there, underneath a **scraggly** tree, in a circle of **bush**es, Edward was dropped in front of a large pair of feet.

The dog began to bark.

Edward looked up and saw that the feet were **attach**ed to an **enormous** man with a long, dark **beard**.

"What's this, Lucy?" said the man.

He bent and picked up Edward. He held him **firm**ly around the middle. "Lucy," said the man, "I know how much you enjoy rabbit pie."

Lucy barked.

"Yes, yes, I know. Rabbit pie is a true **delight**, one of the pleasures of our **existence**."

Lucy let out a hopeful **yip**.

"And what we have here, what you have so **gracious**ly delivered to me, is **definitely** a rabbit, but the best **chef** in the world would be **hard-pressed** to make him into a pie."

Lucy growled.

"This rabbit is made of china, girl." The man held Edward closer to him. They looked each other in the eye. "You're made of china, aren't you, Malone?" He gave Edward a playful shake. "You're some child's toy, am I right? And you have been **separated**, somehow, from the child who loves you."

Edward felt, again, the sharp pain in his chest. He thought of Abilene. He saw the path **lead**ing up to the house on Egypt Street. He saw the **dusk descend**ing and Abilene running toward him.

Yes, Abilene had loved him.

"So, Malone," said the man. He cleared his throat. "You are lost. That is my guess. Lucy and I are lost too."

At the sound of her name, Lucy let out another yip.

"Perhaps," said the man, "you would like to be lost with us. I have found it much more **agreeable** to be lost in the **company** of others. My name is Bull. Lucy, as you may have **surmised**, is my dog. Would you **care** to join us?"

Bull waited for a moment, staring at Edward; and then with his hands still firmly around Edward's waist, the man reached one enormous finger up and touched Edward's head from behind. He pushed it so it looked as if Edward were **nodding** his head in agreement.

"Look, Lucy. He is saying yes," said Bull. "Malone has agreed to travel with us. Isn't that **swell**?"

Lucy danced around Bull's feet, **wagging** her tail and barking.

And so it was that Edward **took to the road** with a **hobo** and his dog.

# Chapter Thirteen

THEY TRAVELED ON FOOT. THEY traveled in empty railcars. They were always on the move.

"But in truth," said Bull, "we are going nowhere. That, my friend, is the **irony** of our **constant** movement."

Edward rode in Bull's **bedroll**, **slung** over Bull's shoulders with only his head and ears **sticking out**. Bull was always careful to **position** the rabbit so that he was not looking down or up, but was, instead, forever looking behind him, at the road they had just traveled.

At night, they slept on the ground, under the stars. Lucy, after her **initial** disappointment about Edward being unfit for **consumption**, took a **liking** to him and slept **curled** up beside him; sometimes she even rested her **muzzle** on his china stomach, and then the noises she made in her sleep, **whimper**ing and **growl**ing and **chuffing**, **resonated** inside Edward's body. To his surprise, he began to feel a deep **tenderness** for the dog.

During the night, while Bull and Lucy slept, Edward, with his ever-open eyes, stared up at the **constellation**s. He said their names, and then he said the names of the people who loved him. He started with Abilene and then went to Nellie and Lawrence and from there to Bull and Lucy, and then he ended again with Abilene: Abilene, Nellie, Lawrence, Bull, Lucy, Abilene.

See? Edward told Pellegrina. I am not like the princess. I know about love.

There were times, too, when Bull and Lucy **gather**ed around a campfire with other **tramp**s. Bull was a good storyteller and an even better singer.

"Sing for us, Bull," the men shouted.

Bull sat with Lucy **lean**ing against his leg and Edward balanced on his right knee and he sang from somewhere deep inside himself. Just as Edward could feel Lucy's whimpers and growls resonate through his body at night, he could also feel the deep, sad sound of Bull's songs move through him. Edward loved it when Bull sang.

And he was grateful to Bull too, for **sensing** that a dress was not the right kind of clothing for Edward.

Edward loved it when Bull sang.

"Malone," said Bull one night, "it's not my desire to **offend** you or to **comment negatively** on your choice of **garb**, but I'm **forced** to tell you that you stick out like a **sore** thumb in that princess dress. And also, again, with no wish to offend you, the dress has seen better days."

Nellie's beautiful dress had not **fared** well at the **dump** or in its **subsequent ramblings** with Bull and Lucy. It was so **torn** and dirty and full of holes that it **barely resembled** a dress any more.

"I have a solution," said Bull, "and I hope that it meets with your **approval**."

He took his own **knit** stocking cap★ and cut a big hole in the top of it and two small holes in either side of it and then he took off Edward's dress.

"Look away, Lucy," he said to the dog, "let's not **embarrass** Malone by staring at his **naked**ness." Bull **slid** the hat over Edward's head and pulled it down and **poked** his arms through the smaller holes. "There you go," he said to Edward. "Now you just need some pants."

The pants Bull made himself, cutting up several red **handkerchiefs** and **sewing** them together so that they formed a **makeshift** covering for Edward's long legs.

---

★ **stocking cap** 스타킹 캡. 끝에 술 등이 달려 있는 원뿔 모양의 털실 모자.

"Now you have the proper **outlaw** look," said Bull, standing back to **admire** his work. "Now you look like a rabbit **on the run**."

# Chapter Fourteen

AT FIRST, THE OTHERS THOUGHT THAT Edward was a great good joke.

"A rabbit," the **hobo**es said, laughing. "Let's **chop** him up and put him in the stew pot.★"

Or when Bull sat with Edward carefully balanced on his knee, one of them would call out, "Got yourself a little dolly,✳ Bull?"

Edward, of course, felt a **surge** of anger at being **refer**red to as a dolly. But Bull never got angry. He simply sat with Edward on his knee and said nothing. Soon the men became **accustom**ed to Edward, and word of his **existence spread**. So it was that when Bull and Lucy

---

★ **stew pot** 양쪽 손잡이가 달린 대형 냄비.
✳ **dolly** (유아어) 인형.

stepped up to a campfire in another town, another state, another place **entirely**, the men knew Edward and were glad to see him.

"Malone!" they shouted in **unison**.

And Edward felt a warm **rush** of pleasure at being **recognized**, at being known.

Whatever it was that had begun in Nellie's kitchen, Edward's new and strange **ability** to sit very still and **concentrate** the whole of his being on the stories of another became **invaluable** around the hobo campfire.

"Look at Malone," said a man named Jack one evening. "He's listening to every dang★ word."

"Certainly," said Bull, "of course he is."

Later that night, Jack came and sat next to Bull and asked if he could **borrow** the rabbit. Bull handed Edward over, and Jack sat with Edward upon his knee. He **whisper**ed in Edward's ear.

"Helen," Jack said, "and Jack Junior and Taffy—she's the baby. Those are my kids' names. They are all in North Carolina. You ever been to North Carolina? It's a pretty state. That's where they are. Helen. Jack Junior. Taffy. You remember their names, okay, Malone?"

After this, wherever Bull and Lucy and Edward

---

★ dang damn의 완곡어. 괘씸한, 넌더리나는.

went, some **tramp** would take Edward **aside** and whisper the names of his children in Edward's ear. Betty. Ted. Nancy. William. Jimmy. Eileen. Skipper. Faith.

Edward knew what it was like to say over and over again the names of those you had left behind. He knew what it was like to miss someone. And so he listened. And in his listening, his heart opened wide and then wider still.

The rabbit stayed lost with Lucy and Bull for a long time. Almost seven years passed, and in that time, Edward became an excellent tramp: happy to be on the road, **restless** when he was still. The sound of the wheels on the train tracks became a music that **soothe**d him. He could have ridden the rails forever. But one night, in a railroad yard in Memphis, as Bull and Lucy slept in an empty **freight** car and Edward kept watch, trouble arrived.

A man entered the freight car and **shone** a **flashlight** in Bull's face and then kicked him awake.

"You **bum**," he said, "you dirty bum. I'm sick of you guys sleeping everywhere. This ain't no motel."

Bull sat up slowly. Lucy started to bark.

"Shut up," said the man. He delivered a **swift** kick to Lucy's side that made her **yelp** in surprise.

All his life, Edward had known what he was: a rabbit

made of china, a rabbit with **bendable** arms and legs and ears. He was bendable, though, only if he was in the hands of another. He could not move himself. And he had never regretted this more deeply than he did that night when he and Bull and Lucy were discovered in the empty railcar. Edward wanted to be able to **defend** Lucy. But he could do nothing. He could only **lie** there and wait.

"Say something," said the man to Bull.

Bull put his hands up in the air. He said, "We are lost."

"Lost, ha. You **bet** you're lost." And then the man said, "What's this?" and he shone the light on Edward.

"That's Malone," said Bull.

"What the heck?★" said the man. He **poked** at Edward with the toe of his boot. "Things are out of control. Things are out of hand. Not on my **watch**. No, sir. Not when I'm in **charge**."

The train suddenly **lurch**ed into motion.

"No, sir," said the man again. He looked down at Edward, "No free rides for rabbits." He turned and **flung** open the door of the railcar, and then he turned back and with one swift kick, and sent Edward sailing out into the

★ heck hell의 완곡어. 이런, 도대체.

darkness.

The rabbit flew through the late spring air.

From far behind him, he heard Lucy's **anguished howl.**

*Arroooooooooo, ahhhhrrrrrrooo*, she cried.

Edward landed with a most alarming ***thump***, and then he **tumbled** and tumbled and tumbled down a long dirty hill. When he finally stopped moving, he was on his back, **staring** up at the night sky. The world was silent. He could not hear Lucy. He could not hear the train.

Edward looked up at the stars. He started to say the names of the constellations, but then he stopped.

Bull, his heart said. Lucy.

How many times, Edward **wondered**, would he have to leave without getting the chance to say goodbye?

A lone **cricket** started up a song.

Edward listened.

Something deep inside him **ached**.

He wished that he could cry.

# Chapter Fifteen

IN THE MORNING, THE SUN ROSE AND the **cricket** song **gave way** to birdsong and an old woman came walking down the dirt road and **trip**ped right over Edward.

"Humph," she said. She pushed at Edward with her fishing **pole**.

"Looks like a rabbit," she said. She put down her basket and bent and stared at Edward. "Only he ain't real."

She stood back up. "Humph," she said again. She **rub**bed her back. "What I say is, there's a use for everything and everything has its use. That's what I say."

Edward didn't care what she said. The terrible **ache** he had felt the night before had gone away and had been **replaced** with a different feeling, one of **hollow**ness and

**despair.**

Pick me up or don't pick me up, the rabbit thought. It makes no difference to me.

The old lady picked him up.

She bent him double and put him in her basket, which smelled of **weeds** and fish, and then she kept walking, **swing**ing the basket and singing, "Nobody knows the troubles I seen."

Edward, **in spite of** himself, listened.

I've seen troubles too, he thought. You **bet** I have. And **apparent**ly they aren't over yet.

Edward was right. His troubles were not over.

The old woman found a use for him.

She **hung** him from a pole in her vegetable garden. She **nail**ed his ears to the wooden pole and spread his arms out as if he were flying and **attach**ed his **paws** to the pole by wrapping pieces of **wire** around them. In addition to Edward, pie **tins** hung from the pole. They **clink**ed and **clanked** and **shone** in the morning sun.

"Ain't a doubt in my mind that you can scare them off," the old lady said.

Scare who off? Edward wondered.

Birds, he soon discovered.

**Crows**. They came flying at him, **cawing** and **screeching**, **wheeling** over his head, diving at his ears.

"Go on, Clyde," said the woman. She **clapped** her hands. "You got to act **ferocious.**"

Clyde? Edward felt a **weariness** so **intense** wash over him that he thought he might actually be able to **sigh aloud**. Would the world never tire of calling him by the wrong name?

The old woman clapped her hands again. "Get to work, Clyde," she said. "Scare them birds off." And then she walked away from him, out of the garden and toward her small house.

The birds were **insistent**. They flew around his head. They **tugged** at the **loose threads** in his sweater. One large crow in **particular** would not leave the rabbit alone. He **perch**ed on the pole and screamed a dark message in Edward's left ear—*Caw, caw, caw*—without **ceasing**. As the sun rose higher and shone **mean**er and brighter, Edward became somewhat **dazed**. He mistook the large crow for Pellegrina.

Go ahead, he thought. Turn me into a warthog if you want. I don't care. I am done with caring.

*Caw, caw,* said the Pellegrina crow.

Finally, the sun set and the birds flew away. Edward hung by his ears and looked up at the night sky. He saw the stars. But for the first time in his life, he looked at them and felt no **comfort**. Instead, he felt **mocked**.

I have been loved, Edward told the stars.

You are down there alone, the stars seemed to say to him. And we are up here, in our **constellations**, together.

I have been loved, Edward told the stars.

So? said the stars. What difference does that make when you are all alone now?

Edward could think of no answer to that question.

Eventually, the sky lightened and the stars disappeared one by one. The birds returned and the old woman came back to the garden.

She brought a boy with her.

# Chapter Sixteen

BRYCE," SAID THE OLD WOMAN, "GIT★ away from that rabbit. I ain't paying you to stand and **stare.**"

"Yes, ma'am," said Bryce. He wiped his nose with the back of his hand and continued to look up at Edward. The boy's eyes were brown with **flecks** of gold shining in them.

"Hey," he **whisper**ed to Edward.

A **crow** settled on Edward's head, and the boy **flap**ped his arms and shouted, "Go on, git!" and the bird **spread** its wings and flew away.

"Bryce!" shouted the old woman.

★ git get의 사투리.

"Ma'am?" said Bryce.

"Git away from that rabbit. Do your work. I ain't gonna say it again."

"Yes'm," said Bryce. He wiped his hand across his nose. "I'll be back to get you," he said to Edward.

The rabbit spent the day hanging by his ears, baking in the hot sun, watching the old woman and Bryce **weed** and **hoe** the garden. Whenever the woman wasn't looking, Bryce raised his hand and waved.

The birds circled over Edward's head, laughing at him.

What was it like to have wings? Edward wondered. If he had had wings when he was tossed **overboard**, he would not have **sunk** to the bottom of the sea. Instead, he would have flown in the **opposite** direction, up, into the deep, bright blue sky. And when Lolly took him to the **dump**, he would have flown out of the **garbage** and followed her and landed on her head, holding on with his sharp **claws**. And on the train, when the man kicked him, Edward would not have fallen to the ground; instead he would have risen up and sat on top of the train and laughed at the man: *Caw, caw, caw.*

In the late afternoon, Bryce and the old lady left the field. Bryce winked at Edward as he walked past him. One of the crows lighted on Edward's shoulder and **tapped** with its **beak** at Edward's china face, **reminding** the rabbit with each tap that he had no wings; that not only could he not fly, he could not move on his own at all, in any way.

**Dusk descend**ed over the field, and then came true dark. A whippoorwill★ sang out over and over again. *Whip poor Will. Whip poor Will.* It was the saddest sound Edward had ever heard. And then came another song, the **hum** of a harmonica.

Bryce stepped out of the shadows.

"Hey," he said to Edward. He wiped his nose with the back of his hand and then played another bit of song on the harmonica. "I **bet** you didn't think I'd come back. But here I am. I come to save you."

Too late, thought Edward as Bryce climbed the pole and worked at the **wires** that were tied around his wrists. I am nothing but a **hollow** rabbit.

Too late, thought Edward as Bryce pulled the **nails** out of his ears. I am only a doll made of china.

But when the last nail was out and he fell forward into Bryce's arms, the rabbit felt a **rush of relief**, and the feeling of relief was followed by one of joy.

Perhaps, he thought, it is not too late, after all, for me to be saved.

---

★ **whippoorwill** [조류] 쏙독새.

# Chapter Seventeen

BRYCE SLUNG EDWARD OVER HIS shoulder. He started to walk.

"I come to get you for Sarah Ruth," Bryce said. "You don't know Sarah Ruth. She's my sister. She's sick. She had her a baby doll made out of china. She loved that baby doll. But he broke it.

"He *broke* it. He was drunk and stepped on that baby's head and smashed it into a hundred million pieces. Them pieces was so small, I couldn't make them go back together. I couldn't. I tried and tried."

At this point in his story, Bryce stopped walking and shook his head and wiped at his nose with the back of his hand.

"Sarah Ruth ain't had nothing to play with since. He

won't buy her nothing. He says she don't need nothing. He says she don't need nothing because she ain't gonna live. But he don't know."

Bryce started to walk again. "He don't know," he said.

Who "he" was was not clear to Edward. What was clear was that he was being taken to a child to make up for the loss of a doll. A doll. How Edward **loathed** dolls. And to be thought of as a likely **replace**ment for a doll **offend**ed him. But still, it was, he had to **admit**, a highly **prefer**able **alternative** to hanging by his ears from a **post**.

The house in which Bryce and Sarah Ruth lived was so small and **crooked** that Edward did not believe, at first, that it was a house. He mistook it, instead, for a chicken **coop**. Inside, there were two beds and a kerosene lamp★ and not much else. Bryce **laid** Edward at the foot of one of the beds and then **lit** the lamp.

"Sarah," Bryce **whisper**ed, "Sarah Ruth. You got to wake up now, honey. I brung you something." He took the harmonica out of his pocket and played the beginning of a simple melody.

The little girl sat up in her bed and **immediately** started to **cough**. Bryce put his hand on her back. "That's

---

★ **kerosene lamp** 등유(kerosene)로 사용하는 램프.

all right," he told her. "That's okay."

She was young, maybe four years old, and she had white-blond hair, and even in the poor light of the lamp, Edward could see that her eyes were the same gold-flecked brown as Bryce's.

"That's right," said Bryce. "You go on ahead and cough."

Sarah Ruth **obliged** him. She coughed and coughed and coughed. On the wall of the **cabin**, the kerosene light **cast** her **trembling** shadow, **hunched** over and small. The coughing was the saddest sound that Edward had ever heard, sadder even than the **mournful** call of the whippoorwill. Finally, Sarah Ruth stopped.

Bryce said, "You want to see what I brung you?"

Sarah Ruth nodded.

"You got to close your eyes."

The girl closed her eyes.

Bryce picked up Edward and held him so that he was standing straight, like a soldier, at the end of the bed. "All right now, you can open them."

Sarah Ruth opened her eyes, and Bryce moved Edward's china legs and china arms so it looked as if he were dancing.

Sarah Ruth laughed and **clapped** her hands. "Rabbit," she said.

"He's for you, honey," said Bryce.

Sarah Ruth looked first at Edward and then at Bryce and then back at Edward again, her eyes wide and disbelieving.

"He's yours."

"Mine?"

Sarah Ruth, Edward was soon to discover, **rarely** said more than one word at a time. Words, at least several of them **strung** together, made her cough. She **limited** herself. She said only what needed to be said.

"Yours," said Bryce. "I got him special for you."

This knowledge **provoked** another **fit** of coughing in Sarah Ruth, and she hunched over again. When the fit was done, she **uncurled** herself and held out her arms.

"That's right," said Bryce. He handed Edward to her.

"Baby," said Sarah Ruth.

She **rocked** Edward back and forth and stared down at him and smiled.

Never in his life had Edward been **cradled** like a baby. Abilene had not done it. Nor had Nellie. And most certainly Bull had not. It was a **singular sensation** to be held so gently and yet so **fiercely**, to be stared down at with so much love. Edward felt the whole of his china body **flood** with warmth.

"You going to give him a name, honey?" Bryce asked.

"Hush," she said to Edward as she rocked him back and forth.

"Jangles," said Sarah Ruth without taking her eyes off Edward.

"Jangles, huh? That's a good name. I like that name."

Bryce **patted** Sarah Ruth on the head. She continued to stare down at Edward.

"**Hush**," she said to Edward as she rocked him back and forth.

"From the minute I first seen him," said Bryce, "I knew he belonged to you. I said to myself, 'That rabbit is for Sarah Ruth, for sure.' "

"Jangles," **murmured** Sarah Ruth.

Outside the cabin, thunder **cracked** and then came the sound of rain falling on the **tin** roof. Sarah Ruth rocked Edward back and forth, back and forth, and Bryce took out his harmonica and started to play, making his song keep rhythm with the rain.

# Chapter Eighteen

BRYCE AND SARAH RUTH HAD A FATHER.

Early the next morning, when the light was gray and uncertain, Sarah Ruth was sitting up in bed, **coughing**, and the father came home. He picked Edward up by one of his ears and said, “I ain’t never.”

“It’s a baby doll,” said Bryce.

“Don’t look like no baby doll to me.”

Edward, hanging by one ear, was **frightened**. This, he was certain, was the man who **crushed** the heads of china dolls.

“Jangles,” said Sarah Ruth between coughs. She held out her arms.

“He’s hers,” said Bryce. “He belongs to her.”

The father dropped Edward on the bed, and Bryce

picked up the rabbit and handed him to Sarah Ruth.

"It don't matter anyway," said the father. "It don't make no difference. None of it."

"It does so matter," said Bryce.

"Don't you **sass** me," said the father. He raised his hand and **slap**ped Bryce across his mouth and then he turned and left the house.

"You ain't got to worry about him," said Bryce to Edward. "He ain't nothing but a **bully**. And besides, he don't **hardly** ever come home."

**Fortunately**, the father did not come back that day. Bryce went out to work and Sarah Ruth spent the day in bed, holding Edward in her **lap** and playing with a box filled with buttons.

"Pretty," she said to Edward as she lined up the buttons on the bed and **arrange**d them into different patterns.

Sometimes, when a coughing **fit** was **particular**ly bad, she **squeezed** Edward so tight that he was afraid he would crack in two. Also, in between coughing fits, she took to **suck**ing on one or the other of Edward's ears. Normally, Edward would have found **intrusive**, **clingy** behavior of this **sort** very **annoy**ing, but there was something about Sarah Ruth. He wanted to take care of her. He wanted to **protect** her. He wanted to do *more* for her.

At the end of the day, Bryce returned with a **biscuit** for Sarah Ruth and a ball of **twine** for Edward.

Sarah Ruth held the biscuit in both hands and took small, **tentative** bites.

"You eat that all up, honey. Let me hold Jangles," said Bryce. "Him and me got a surprise for you."

Bryce took Edward off to a corner of the room, and with his pocket knife, he cut off lengths of twine and tied them to Edward's arms and feet and then tied the twine to sticks of wood.

"See, all day I been thinking about it," Bryce said, "what we're going to do is make you dance. Sarah Ruth loves dancing. Mama used to hold on to her and dance her around the room.

"You eating that biscuit?" Bryce called out to Sarah Ruth.

"Uh-huh," said Sarah Ruth.

"You hold on, honey. We got a surprise for you." Bryce stood up. "Close your eyes," he told her. He took Edward over to the bed and said, "Okay, you can open them now."

Sarah Ruth opened her eyes.

"Dance, Jangles," said Bryce. And then, moving the strings with the sticks with his one hand, Bryce made Edward dance and drop and **sway**. And the whole while, at the same time, with his other hand, he held on to the harmonica and played a bright and **lively tune**.

Sarah Ruth laughed. She laughed until she started to cough, and then Bryce **laid** Edward down and took Sarah Ruth in his lap and **rock**ed her and **rub**bed her back.

"You want some fresh air?" he asked her. "Let's get you out of this **nasty** old air, huh?"

Bryce carried his sister outside. He left Edward **lying** on the bed; and the rabbit, **staring** up at the smoke-**stain**ed ceiling, thought again about having wings. If he had them, he thought, he would fly high above the world, to where the air was clear and sweet, and he would take Sarah Ruth with him. He would carry her in his arms. Surely, so high above the world, she would be able to breathe without coughing.

After a minute, Bryce came back inside, still carrying Sarah Ruth.

"She wants you too," he said.

"Jangles," said Sarah Ruth. She held out her arms.

So Bryce held Sarah Ruth and Sarah Ruth held Edward and the three of them stood outside.

Bryce said, "You got to look for falling stars. Them are the ones with magic."

They were quiet for a long time, all three of them looking up at the sky. Sarah Ruth stopped coughing.

Edward thought that maybe she had fallen asleep.

"There," she said. And she pointed to a star streaking through the night sky.

"Make a wish, honey," Bryce said, his voice high and tight. "That's your star. You make you a wish for anything you want."

And even though it was Sarah Ruth's star, Edward wished on it too.

# Chapter Nineteen

THE DAYS PASSED. THE SUN ROSE AND set and rose and set again and again. Sometimes the father came home and sometimes he did not. Edward's ears became **soggy** and he did not care. His sweater had almost completely **unravel**ed and it didn't bother him. He was hugged half to death and it felt good. In the evenings, at the hands of Bryce, at the ends of the **twine**, Edward danced and danced.

One month passed and then two and then three. Sarah Ruth got worse. In the fifth month, she **refused** to eat. And in the sixth month, she began to **cough** up blood. Her breathing became **ragged** and uncertain, as if she was trying to remember, in between breaths, what to do, what breathing was.

"Breathe, honey," Bryce stood over her and said.

Breathe, thought Edward from deep inside the well of her arms. Please, please breathe.

Bryce stopped leaving the house. He sat at home all day and held Sarah Ruth in his lap and rocked her back and forth and sang to her; on a bright morning in September, Sarah Ruth stopped breathing.

"Oh no," said Bryce. "Oh, honey, take a little breath. Please."

Edward had fallen out of Sarah Ruth's arms the night before and she had not asked for him again. So, face down on the floor, arms over his head, Edward listened as Bryce wept. He listened as the father came home and shouted at Bryce. He listened as the father wept.

"You can't cry!" Bryce shouted. "You got no right to cry. You never even loved her. You don't know nothing about love."

"I loved her," said the father. "I loved her."

I loved her too, thought Edward. I loved her and now she is gone. How could this be, he wondered. How could he bear to live in a world without Sarah Ruth?

The yelling between the father and son continued, and then there was a terrible moment when the father insisted that Sarah Ruth belonged to him, that she was his girl, his baby, and that he was taking her to be buried.

"Come on, Jangles,"

"She ain't yours!" Bryce screamed. "You can't take her. She ain't yours."

But the father was bigger and stronger, and he **prevailed**. He wrapped Sarah Ruth in a **blanket** and carried her away. The small house became very quiet. Edward could hear Bryce moving around, **muttering** to himself. And then, finally, the boy picked Edward up.

"Come on, Jangles," Bryce said. "We're leaving. We're going to Memphis."

# CHAPTER TWENTY

HOW MANY DANCING RABBITS HAVE you seen in your life?" Bryce said to Edward. "I can tell you how many I seen. One. You. That's how you and me are going to make some money. I seen it the last time I was in Memphis. Folks put on any kind of show right there on the street corner and people pay 'em for it. I seen it."

The walk to town took all night. Bryce walked without stopping, carrying Edward under one arm and talking to him the whole time. Edward tried to listen, but the terrible scarecrow feeling had come back, the feeling he had when he was hanging by his ears in the old lady's garden, the feeling that nothing mattered, and that nothing would ever matter again.

And not only did Edward feel **hollow**; he **ached**. Every part of his china body hurt. He ached for Sarah Ruth. He wanted her to hold him. He wanted to dance for her.

And he did dance, but it was not for Sarah Ruth. Edward danced for strangers on a dirty street corner in Memphis. Bryce played his harmonica and moved Edward's **strings**, and Edward **bowed** and **shuffled** and **swayed** and people stopped to **stare** and point and laugh. On the ground in front of them was Sarah Ruth's button box. The **lid** was open to **encourage** people to drop **change** inside it.

"Mama," said a small child, "look at that bunny. I want to touch him." He reached out his hand for Edward.

"No," said the mother, "dirty." She pulled the child back, away from Edward. "**Nasty**," she said.

A man wearing a hat stopped and stared at Edward and Bryce.

"It's a **sin** to dance," he said. And then after a long **pause**, he said, "It's a **particular** sin for rabbits to dance."

The man took off his hat and held it over his heart. He stood and watched the boy and the rabbit for a long time. Finally, he put his hat back on his head and walked away.

The shadows **lengthened**. The sun became an orange

**dust**y ball low in the sky. Bryce started to cry. Edward saw his tears land on the **pavement**. But the boy did not stop playing his harmonica. He did not make Edward stop dancing.

An old woman **lean**ing on a **cane** stepped up close to them. She stared at Edward with deep, dark eyes.

Pellegrina? thought the dancing rabbit.

She **nod**ded at him.

Look at me, he said to her. His arms and legs **jerk**ed. Look at me. You got your wish. I have learned how to love. And it's a terrible thing. I'm broken. My heart is broken. Help me.

The old woman turned and **hobbl**ed away.

Come back, thought Edward. Fix me.

Bryce cried harder. He made Edward dance faster.

Finally, when the sun was gone and the streets were dark, Bryce stopped playing his harmonica.

"I'm done now," he said.

He let Edward fall to the pavement. "I ain't gonna cry any more." Bryce wiped his nose and his eyes with the back of his hand; he picked up the button box and looked inside it. "We got us enough money to get something to eat," he said. "Come on, Jangles."

# Chapter Twenty-One

THE DINER WAS CALLED NEAL'S. THE word was written in big, red neon letters that flashed on and off. Inside, it was warm and bright and smelled like fried chicken and toast and coffee.

Bryce sat at the counter and put Edward on a stool next to him. He leaned the rabbit's forehead up against the counter so that he would not fall.

"What you gonna have, sugar?" the waitress said to Bryce.

"Give me some pancakes," said Bryce, "and some eggs, and I want steak too. I want a big old steak. And some toast. And some coffee."

The waitress leaned forward and pulled at one of Edward's ears and then pushed him backward so that she could see his face.

"This your rabbit?" she said to Bryce.

"Yes'm. He's mine now. He belonged to my sister." Bryce wiped his nose with the back of his hand. "We're in show business, me and him."

"Is that right?" said the waitress. She had a name tag on the front of her dress. *Marlene* it said. She looked at Edward's face, and then she let go of his ear and he fell forward so that his head rested against the counter again.

Go ahead, Marlene, thought Edward. Push me around. Do with me as you will. What does it matter? I am broken. Broken.

The food came, and Bryce ate all of it without even looking up from his plate.

"Well, you was hungry for sure," said Marlene as she cleared away the plates. "I **reckon** show business is hard work."

"Yes'm," said Bryce.

Marlene **tucked** the **check** under the coffee cup. Bryce picked it up and looked at it and then shook his head.

"I ain't got enough," he said to Edward.

"Ma'am," he said to Marlene when she came back and filled up his coffee cup, "I ain't got enough."

"What, sugar?"

"I ain't got enough money."

She stopped pouring the coffee and looked at him. "You're going to have to talk to Neal about that."

Neal, it turned out, was both the owner and the cook. He was a large, red-haired, red-faced man who came out of the kitchen holding a **spatula** in one hand.

"You came in here hungry, right?" he said to Bryce.

"Yes, sir," said Bryce. He wiped his nose with the back of his hand.

"And you ordered some food and I cooked it and Marlene brought it to you. Right?"

"I reckon," said Bryce.

"You reckon?" said Neal. He brought the spatula down on the counter with a ***thwack***.

Bryce jumped. "Yes, sir. I mean, no sir."

"I. Cooked. It. For. You," said Neal.

"Yes, sir," said Bryce. He picked Edward up off the stool and held him close. Everyone in the diner had stopped eating. They were all staring at the boy and the rabbit and Neal. Only Marlene looked away.

"You ordered it. I cooked it. Marlene **served** it. You ate it. Now," said Neal. "I want my money." He **tapped** the spatula lightly on the counter.

Bryce cleared his **throat**. "You ever seen a rabbit dance?" he said.

"How's that?" said Neal.

"You ever before in your life seen a rabbit dance?" Bryce set Edward on the floor and started pulling the **strings attach**ed to his feet, making him do a slow **shuffle.** He put his harmonica in his mouth and played a sad song that went along with the dance.

Somebody laughed.

Bryce took the harmonica out of his mouth and said, "He could dance some more if you want him to. He could dance to pay for what I ate."

Neal stared at Bryce. And then without **warn**ing, he reached down and **grab**bed hold of Edward.

"This is what I think of dancing rabbits," said Neal. And he **swung** Edward by the feet, swung him so that his head hit the **edge** of the counter hard.

There was a loud **crack.**

Bryce screamed.

And the world, Edward's world, went black.

# Chapter Twenty-two

IT WAS **DUSK**, AND EDWARD WAS WALKING down a **sidewalk**. He was walking on his own, putting one foot in front of the other without any **assistance** from anybody. He was wearing a fine suit made of red silk.

He walked down the sidewalk, and then he turned onto a path that **led** up to a house with lighted windows.

I know this house, thought Edward. This is Abilene's house. I am on Egypt Street.

Lucy came running out of the front door of the house, barking and jumping and **wagging** her tail.

"Down, girl," said a deep, **gruff** voice.

Edward looked up and there was Bull, standing at the door.

"Hello, Malone," said Bull. "Hello, good old rabbit pie. We've been waiting for you." Bull swung the door wide and Edward walked inside.

Abilene was there, and Nellie and Lawrence and Bryce.

"Susanna," called Nellie.

"Jangles," said Bryce.

"Edward," said Abilene. She held out her arms to him.

But Edward stood still. He looked around the room.

"You searching for Sarah Ruth?" Bryce asked.

Edward **nod**ded.

"You got to go outside if you want to see Sarah Ruth," said Bryce.

So they all went outside, Lucy and Bull and Nellie and Lawrence and Bryce and Abilene and Edward.

"Right there," said Bryce. He pointed up at the stars.

"Yep," said Lawrence, "that is the Sarah Ruth **constellation**." He picked Edward up and put him on his shoulder. "You can see it right there."

Edward felt a **pang** of **sorrow**, deep and sweet and **familiar**. Why did she have to be so far away?

If only I had wings, he thought, I could fly to her.

Out of the corner of his eye, the rabbit saw something **flutter**. Edward looked over his shoulder and there they were, the most **magnificent** wings he had ever seen, orange and red and blue and yellow. And they were on his back. They belonged to him. They were his wings.

What a wonderful night this was! He was walking on his own. He had an **elegant** new suit. And now he had wings. He could fly anywhere, do anything. Why had he never realized it before?

His heart **soar**ed inside of him. He **spread** his wings and flew off Lawrence's shoulders, out of his hands and up into the night time sky, toward the stars, toward Sarah Ruth.

"No!" shouted Abilene.

"Catch him," said Bryce.

Edward flew higher.

Lucy barked.

"Malone!" shouted Bull. And with a **terrific lunge**, he **grab**bed hold of Edward's feet and pulled him out of the sky and **wrestle**d him to the earth. "You can't go yet," said Bull.

"Stay with us," said Abilene.

Edward **beat** his wings, but it was no use. Bull held him **firm**ly to the ground.

"Stay with us," repeated Abilene.

Edward started to cry.

"I couldn't **stand** to lose him again," said Nellie.

"Neither could I," said Abilene. "It would break my heart."

Lucy bent her face to Edward's.

She licked his tears away.

# Chapter Twenty-three

EXCEEDINGLY WELL MADE—," SAID THE man who was running a warm **cloth** over Edward's face, "a work of art, I would say—a **surpassingly**, unbelievably dirty work of art, but art **nonetheless**. And dirt can be **dealt** with. Just as your broken head has been dealt with."

Edward looked into the eyes of the man.

"Ah, there you are," the man said. "I can see that you are listening now. Your head was broken. I fixed it. I brought you back from the world of the dead."

My heart, thought Edward, my *heart* is broken.

"No, no. No need to thank me," the man said. "It's my job, quite **literally**. Allow me to introduce myself. I am Lucius Clarke, doll **mender**. Your head . . . may I tell you? Will it **upset** you? Well, I always say the truth must be met **head-on**, no **pun intend**ed. Your head, young sir, was in twenty-one pieces."

Twenty-one pieces? Edward repeated **mindless**ly.

Lucius Clarke nodded. "Twenty-one," he said. "All **modesty aside**, I must **admit** that a lesser doll mender, a doll mender without my skills, might not have been able to **rescue** you. But let's not speak of what might have been. Let us speak instead of what is. You are **whole**. You have been pulled back from the **brink** of **oblivion** by your **humble servant**, Lucius Clarke." And here, Lucius Clarke put his hand on his chest and **bow**ed deeply over Edward.

This was quite a speech to wake up to, and Edward **lay** on his back trying to **absorb** it. He was on a wooden table. He was in a room with sunshine pouring in from high windows. His head, **apparent**ly, had been in twenty-one pieces and now was put back together into one. He was not wearing a red suit. In fact, he had no clothes on at all. He was **naked** again. And he did not have wings.

And then he remembered: Bryce, the **diner**, Neal swinging him through the air.

Bryce.

"You are **wonder**ing, perhaps, about your young friend," said Lucius, "the one with the continually running nose. Yes. He brought you here, **weep**ing,

**begging** for my **assistance**. 'Put him together again,' he said. 'Put him back together.'

"I told him, I said, 'Young sir, I am a businessman. I can put your rabbit back together again. For a price. The question is, can you pay this price?' He could not. Of course, he could not. He said that he could not.

"I told him then that he had two **options**. Only two. The first option being that he seek assistance elsewhere. Option two was that I would fix you to the very best of my **considerable abilities** and then you would become mine—his no longer, but mine."

Here Lucius fell silent. He nodded, agreeing with himself. "Two options only," he said. "And your friend chose option two. He gave you up so that you could be **healed**. **Extraordinary**, really."

Bryce, thought Edward.

Lucius Clarke **clapped** his hands together. "But no worries, my friend. No worries. I fully intend to keep up my end of the **bargain**. I will **restore** you to what I **perceive** to be your former **glory**. You shall have rabbit-fur ears and a rabbit-fur tail. Your **whiskers** will be **repair**ed and **replaced**, your eyes repainted to a bright and **stun**ning blue. You will be clothed in the finest of suits.

"And then, some day, I will **reap** the return on my **investment** in you. All in good time. All in good time. In the doll business, we have a saying: there is real time and there is doll time. You, my fine friend, have entered doll time."

# Chapter Twenty-four

AND SO EDWARD TULANE WAS **MENDED**, put together again, cleaned and **polish**ed, dressed in an **elegant** suit and placed on a high shelf for **display**. From this shelf, Edward could see the whole shop: Lucius Clarke's **workbench** and the windows to the outside world and the door that the customers used to enter and leave. From this shelf, Edward saw Bryce open the door one day and stand on the **threshold**, the silver harmonica in his left hand **flash**ing **brilliant**ly in the sunlight **flood**ing in through the windows.

"Young sir," said Lucius, "I am afraid that we made a **deal**."

"Can't I see him?" asked Bryce. He wiped his hand across his nose and the gesture filled Edward with a terrible feeling of love and loss. "I just want to look at him."

Lucius Clarke **sigh**ed. "You may look," he said. "You may look and then you must go and not come back. I cannot have you in my shop every day **moon**ing over what you have lost."

"Yes, sir," said Bryce.

Lucius sighed again. He got up from his workbench and went to Edward's shelf and picked him up and held him so that Bryce could see him.

"Hey, Jangles," said Bryce. "You look good. The last time I seen you, you looked terrible, your head was **bust**ed in and—"

"He is put together again," said Lucius, "as I promised you he would be."

Bryce nodded. He wiped his hand across his nose.

"Can I hold him?" he asked.

"No," said Lucius.

Bryce nodded again.

"Tell him goodbye," said Lucius Clarke. "He is **repair**ed. He has been saved. Now you must tell him goodbye."

"Goodbye," said Bryce.

Don't go, thought Edward. I won't be able to **bear** it if you go.

"You may look and then you must go and not come back."

"And now you must leave," said Lucius Clarke.

"Yes, sir," said Bryce. But he stood without moving, looking at Edward.

"Go," said Lucius Clarke, "go."

Please, thought Edward, don't.

Bryce turned. He walked through the door of the doll **mender**'s shop. The door closed. The bell **tinkled**.

And Edward was alone.

# Chapter Twenty-five

TECHNICALLY, OF COURSE, HE WAS NOT alone. Lucius Clarke's shop was filled with dolls—lady dolls and baby dolls, dolls with eyes that opened and closed and dolls with painted-on eyes, dolls dressed as queens and dolls wearing **sailor** suits.

Edward had never cared for dolls. He found them **annoying** and **self-centered**, **twitter**y and **vain**. This opinion was **immediately reinforce**d by his first shelf-mate, a china doll with green glass eyes and red lips and dark brown hair. She was wearing a green satin★ dress that fell to her knees.

"What are *you*?" she said in a **high-pitched** voice when

---

★ **satin** 새틴. 광택이 있고 매끄러운 직물.

Edward was placed on the shelf next to her.

"I am a rabbit," said Edward.

The doll let out a small **squeak**. "You're in the wrong place," she said. "This is a shop for dolls. Not rabbits."

Edward said nothing.

"**Shoo**," said the doll.

"I would love to shoo," said Edward, "but it is **obvious** that I cannot."

After a long silence, the doll said, "I hope you don't think that anyone is going to buy you."

Again, Edward said nothing.

"The people who come in here want dolls, not rabbits. They want baby dolls or **elegant** dolls such as myself, dolls with pretty dresses, dolls with eyes that open and close."

"I have no interest in being **purchased**," said Edward.

The doll **gasped**. "You don't want somebody to buy you?" she said. "You don't want to be owned by a little girl who loves you?"

Sarah Ruth! Abilene! Their names went through Edward's head like the **notes** of a sad, sweet song.

"I have already been loved," said Edward. "I have been loved by a girl named Abilene. I have been loved by a fisherman and his wife and a **hobo** and his dog. I have been loved by a boy who played the harmonica and by a girl who died. Don't talk to me about love," he said. "I have known love."

This **impassioned** speech shut up Edward's shelf-mate for a **considerable** amount of time.

"Well," she said at last, "still. My point is that no one is going to buy you."

They did not speak to each other again. The doll was sold two weeks later to a grandmother who was purchasing her for a grandchild. "Yes," she said to Lucius Clarke, "that one right there, the one with the green dress. She is quite lovely."

"Yes," said Lucius, "she is, isn't she?" And he **pluck**ed the doll from the shelf.

Goodbye and **good riddance**, thought Edward.

The **spot** next to the rabbit stayed **vacant** for some time. Day after day, the door to the shop opened and closed, letting in early morning sun or late afternoon light, lifting the hearts of the dolls inside, all of them thinking when the door **swung** wide that this time, this time, the person entering the shop would be the one who wanted them.

Edward was the lone **contrarian**. He **pride**d himself on not hoping, on not allowing his heart to lift inside of him. He prided himself on keeping his heart silent, **immobile**, closed tight.

I am done with hope, thought Edward Tulane.

And then one day at **dusk**, right before he closed the shop, Lucius Clarke placed another doll on the shelf next to Edward.

# Chapter Twenty-six

THERE YOU ARE, MILADY.* MEET THE rabbit doll," said Lucius.

The doll **mender** walked away, turning out the lights one by one.

In the **gloom** of the shop, Edward could see that the doll's head, like his, had been broken and **repair**ed. Her face was, in fact, a web of **cracks**. She was wearing a baby **bonnet**.

"How do you do?" she said in a high, thin voice. "I am pleased to make your **acquaintance**."

"Hello," said Edward.

"Have you been here long?" she asked.

---

* **milady** 마님. 영국 귀부인에 대한 호칭.

"Months and months," said Edward. "But I don't care. One place is the same as another to me."

"Oh, not for me," said the doll. "I have lived one hundred years. And in that time, I have been in places that were **heavenly** and others that were **horrid**. After a time, you learn that each place is different. And you become a different doll in each place too. Quite different."

"One hundred years?" said Edward.

"I am old. The doll mender **confirm**ed this. He said as he was **mend**ing me that I am at least that. At least one hundred. At least one hundred years old."

Edward thought about everything that had happened to him in his short life. What kind of **adventures** would you have if you were in the world for a **century**?

The old doll said, "I **wonder** who will come for me this time. Someone will come. Someone always comes. Who will it be?"

"I don't care if anyone comes for me," said Edward.

"But that's **dreadful**," said the old doll. "There's no point in going on if you feel that way. No point at all. You must be filled with **expectancy**. You must be **awash** in hope. You must wonder who will love you, whom you will love next."

"I am done with being loved," Edward told her. "I'm

done with loving. It's too painful."

"Pish,★" said the old doll. "Where is your **courage**?"

"Somewhere else, I guess," said Edward.

"You disappoint me," she said. "You disappoint me greatly. If you have no **intention** of loving or being loved, then the whole **journey** is **pointless**. You might as well **leap** from this shelf right now and let yourself **shatter** into a million pieces. **Get it over with**. Get it all over with now."

"I would leap if I were able," said Edward.

"Shall I push you?" said the old doll.

"No, thank you," Edward said to her. "Not that you could," he **mutter**ed to himself.

"What's that?"

"Nothing," said Edward.

The dark in the doll shop was now complete. The old doll and Edward sat on their shelf and **stare**d straight ahead.

"You disappoint me," said the old doll.

Her words made Edward think of Pellegrina: of warthogs and princesses, of listening and love, of **spell**s and **curses**. What if there *was* somebody waiting to love him? What if there was somebody whom he would love

★ **pish** 불쾌함을 나타내는 말. 흥, 체.

again? Was it possible?

Edward felt his heart **stir**.

No, he told his heart. Not possible. Not possible.

In the morning, Lucius Clarke came and unlocked the shop, "Good morning, my darlings," he called out to them. "Good morning, my lovelies." He pulled up the **shades** on the windows. He turned on the light over his tools. He **switch**ed the sign on the door to open.

The first customer was a little girl with her father.

"Are you looking for something special?" Lucius Clarke said to them.

"Yes," said the girl, "I am looking for a friend."

Her father put her on his shoulders and they walked slowly around the shop. The girl studied each doll carefully. She looked Edward right in the eye. She **nod**ded at him.

"Have you decided, Natalie?" her father asked.

"Yes," she said, "I want the one in the baby bonnet."

"Oh," said Lucius Clarke, "you know that she is very old. She is an **antique**."

"She needs me," said Natalie **firm**ly.

Next to Edward, the old doll let out a **sigh**. She seemed to sit up straighter. Lucius came and took her off the shelf and handed her to Natalie. And when they left, when the girl's father opened the door for his daughter

Edward's heart stirred.

and the old doll, a bright **shaft** of early morning light came **flood**ing in, and Edward heard quite clearly, as if she were still sitting next to him, the old doll's voice.

"Open your heart," she said gently. "Someone will come. Someone will come for you. But first you must open your heart."

The door closed. The sunlight disappeared.

*Someone will come.*

Edward's heart stirred. He thought, for the first time in a long time, of the house on Egypt Street and of Abilene **wind**ing his watch and then **bend**ing toward him and placing it on his left leg, saying: "I will come home to you."

No, no, he told himself. Don't believe it. Don't let yourself believe it.

But it was too late.

*Someone will come for you.*

The china rabbit's heart had begun, again, to open.

# Chapter Twenty-seven

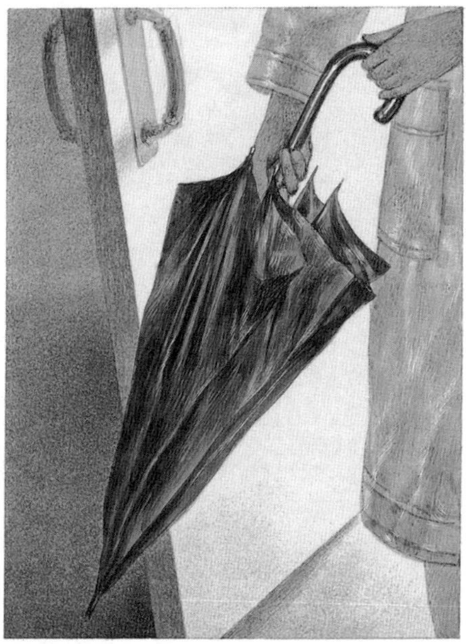

SEASONS PASSED, FALL AND WINTER AND spring and summer. Leaves blew in through the open door of Lucius Clarke's shop, and rain, and the green **outrageous** hopeful light of spring. People came and went, grandmothers and doll **collectors** and little girls with their mothers.

Edward Tulane waited.

The seasons turned into years.

Edward Tulane waited.

He repeated the old doll's words over and over until they **wore** a **smooth groove** of hope in his brain: *Someone will come. Someone will come for you.*

And the old doll was right.

Someone did come.

It was springtime. It was raining. There were dogwood★ **blossom**s on the floor of Lucius Clarke's shop.

She was a small girl, maybe five years old, and while her mother **struggle**d to close a blue umbrella, the little girl walked around the store, stopping and **staring** **solemn**ly at each doll and then moving on.

When she came to Edward, she stood in front of him for what seemed like a long time. She looked at him and he looked back at her.

*Someone will come*, Edward said. *Someone will come for me.*

The girl smiled and then she stood on her tiptoes and took Edward off the shelf. She **cradle**d him in her arms. She held him in the same **ferocious**, **tender** way Sarah Ruth had held him.

Oh, thought Edward, I remember this.

"Madam," said Lucius Clarke, "could you please **attend** to your daughter. She is holding a very **fragile**, very **precious**, quite expensive doll."

"Maggie," said the woman. She looked up from the still-open umbrella. "What have you got?"

"A rabbit," said Maggie.

"A what?" said the mother.

---

★ **dogwood** [식물] 층층나무.

"A rabbit," said Maggie again. "I want him."

"Remember, we're not buying anything today. We're looking only," said the woman.

"Madam," said Lucius Clarke, "please."

The woman came and stood over Maggie. She looked down at Edward.

The rabbit felt **dizzy**.

He **wondered**, for a minute, if his head had **cracked** open again, if he was dreaming.

"Look, Mama," said Maggie, "look at him."

"I see him," said the woman.

She dropped the umbrella. She put her hand on the locket* that **hung** around her neck. And Edward saw then that it was not a locket at all. It was a watch, a pocket watch.

It was his watch.

"Edward?" said Abilene.

Yes, said Edward.

"Edward," she said again, certain this time.

Yes, said Edward, yes, yes, yes.

It's me.

---

★ **locket** 로켓. 사진이나 머리카락 등 기념품을 넣을 수 있도록 목걸이에 다는 작은 갑.

# CODA

ONCE, THERE WAS A CHINA RABBIT who was loved by a little girl. The rabbit went on an ocean **journey** and fell **overboard** and was **rescued** by a fisherman. He was **buried** under **garbage** and unburied by a dog. He traveled for a long time with the **hoboes** and worked for a short time as a **scarecrow**.

Once, there was a rabbit who loved a little girl and watched her die.

The rabbit danced on the streets of Memphis. His head was broken open in a **diner** and was put together again by a doll **mender**.

And the rabbit **swore** that he would not make the mistake of loving again.

Once, there was a rabbit who danced in a garden

in springtime with the daughter of the woman who had loved him at the beginning of his journey. The girl **swung** the rabbit as she danced in circles. Sometimes they went so fast, the two of them, that it seemed as if they were flying. Sometimes it seemed as if they both had wings.

Once, oh **marvelous** once, there was a rabbit who found his way home.